Instructions from a Weaver Bird

Poems by
JONATHAN HILL

buffalomouse books

Instructions from a Weaver Bird

Published in Great Britain by
Buffalomouse Books

email: editor@buffalomousebooks.com
www.buffalomousebooks.com

ISBN: 978-1-9165034-4-1

Cover Design by Clifford Hayes
Cover Illustration by Clare-Marie Edwards

Printed by AnchorPrint Group Ltd

Dedications

For my family
Bernadette-Clare Hill
Clare-Marie Edwards
Martyn-John Hill
and my poetry mentor
Deborah Tyler-Bennett

Acknowledgements

Acknowledgements are due to editors of the following publications in which earlier versions of some of my work appeared:

Writers' Forum (competitions – two prizes). Ware Poets 20th competition anthology. Coffee House Anthology. Rethink your Mind NHS competition Anthology. Old Curiosity Bookshop, Hathern – First Book of Short Stories. WEA and Leicester Museum and Art Gallery Competition prize. Loughborough Echo several poems of the week. WEA East Midlands anthologies. Wolverhampton Municipal Grammar School Old Pupils Association.

Contents

Introductory
Poem

Writer's notebook

Page after page of spiral bound graffiti,
Empty spaces spray painted in
 blood, ink, sweat, tears, or buttered crumbs
from mid-morning breakfast

notebook cover an abstract swirl in
jet black, intense as japanned enamel
 clunky couplets concealed from critical analysis
embryonic sonnets lacking syllables and turns

found verse, flaming slogans, epigrams, gossip
from Arriva bus to Leicester St Margaret's
comedian's catch phrase, circa early sixties,
gushing reminiscences of adolescent ecstasies

fragments of truth, loss, despair and delight,
mental health dialogues between adult and child,
carry notebook three miles, incubate, incubate,
turn new page, playfully create.

Jonathan Hill

Father's advice ignored

Biscuits

How I envied nextdoor's dog
not for his breath, you'll understand,
but for his easy popularity
among the local kids

Amber eyes, camel coat, white-tipped tail,
awareness bristling hair by shiny hair,
eyebrows - horizontal question marks
above a fang-filled smile

Four kinds of bark, all he knew,
they encompassed everything:
joy, suspicion, rage and pain
no need for further self-expression

Daily I rehearsed those barks
to emulate his point of view
attract attention.

Lick a dog biscuit to know
..why chocolate hob-knobs fed
 his sweetest dreams.

Jonathan Hill

Coffee Break 1953

Shush!

Mother's reading Woman's Own
Camp Coffee balanced on her knee
irritating knitting pattern in her lap
perfect scones and tarts to bake for tea.

tales of nurses healing doctors
air hostesses landing airline pilots
dutiful princess - 'coronated'
handsome sun-tanned sailor earning stripes.

Recipes to grow new bonnie babies
(corsets - support the fallen figure)
Silvikrin for glossy hair, shining teeth by Colgate
(etiquette for entertaining, de riguer)

most closely read, the readers' problems page
will others' worries leave Mum feeling better?

Shush!

The Ballad of Jimmy the Chin

When I was a boy with a curious mind
Jimmy the Chin was a man I observed.
His self-given task (no-one else would employ him)
to find chucked out boxes with nothing much in them.

We were scared stiff of Jimmy his jawbone so long
and beady black eyes set deep in his bonce.
When he walked, his nose pecked in time with his knees,
his baggy blue mack shone silky with grease.

"Worro Jimmy," we'd shout, "yo' ygoin' to market?"
Best days of his week, Wednesdays and Sat'days.
When church bells chimed four over half empty stalls
he'd grab armfuls of boxes and take to his heels.

We followed him home just to see where he lived.
A dreadful dank cellar, hard truth that was learned,
we peered through the grime and the half-light inside
saw Jim and his Mom relaxing in chairs.

Crate wood was the fabric from which they were fashioned
And tea chests the tables to lay chipped tin plates on.
Alcoves stacked deep with boxes and cardboard,
bed in each corner, from palettes and hardboard.

Jim's Mom's legs were bandaged from ankle to knee.
"She looks proper poorly," said my mate to me.
Shamefaced we shrank back from that desolate scene
Not returning again to stalk Jimmy the Chin.

Jonathan Hill

One day at our back gate a long scraggy hand
reached over and groped for the rickety latch.
Jim stole into our yard, past toilet and coalhouse,
his search for more boxes had led to our doorstep.

Our Dad was mild mannered, on Jimmy's intrusion,
yelled out a cruel word (beginning with B)
"Boxes", he roared. Jim started to flee.

And I ponder now, as I wondered back then,
What Jim told his Mom, once he'd buggered off wum?
Would he tell her "people were more good than bad
but they'd all sworn at him" as did our Dad?

In the river

To Bridgnorth on a double decker bus,
slender dace the prey and thick-lipped chub,
concealed beneath Sabrina's ribbonned hair.

Hair blonde and green with yellow flecks,
anglers call it water weed, yet
fish lie low in tangled, trailing

strands, defence against
lines, nets and grubby grasping hands
manipulated from the bank by bug-eyed boys.

Sparse catch at lunchtime, nothing much to show,
only in the keep a brace of big-gobgudgeon
and an anxious shoal of manic minnow.

Young fishers trawl all day and eat well too,
silver sardine sarnies, tea well-stewed,
sodden socks laid to bake in sun.

 No luck until lads land the strangest fish
its spine a threatening thorny dorsal fin.
no dark bars but muted spots the camouflage.

Close examination, then return to swim,
once home, consult an illustrated book
 on fish from British rivers, streams and lakes….

 Identify today's prize catch: it's called a Pope or Ruffe,
rather scarce and rarely fished for, much.

Jonathan Hill

Catch of the day

February by silver Severn,
Fishing deep from shimmering shingle drifts.
As dusk fell a pristine Rudd was hooked,
Tinted fins flagged sacrificial red.

Jaws agape a powerful Pike quick struck.
Pierced and paralysed,
our Rudd was quick-reeled in -
predator sank back to river depths.

"We'll take revenge on Mr Pike!" said
Uncle Jack. A bigger hook impaled
 dead Rudd to make a lure. With stronger
line and heavier rod we tantalised sharp teeth.

Temptation hooked the hunter,
hard tug, long pull, landed and despatched -
heavy crack on back of bony skull
home came the corpse. Pausing to sigh,
 mother agreed to clean and gut.

Next door lived Granny Varja from Ukraine
her ancient recipe resurrected
cotton wool, laced with needles –
now at last our fragrant supper!

In prayerful gratitude
Neighbour Varja took the larger share.
Loyally licking lips father wolfed his bait.
Mother shared her portion with our tabby cat
Which, with disdainful grace, tip toed
past fresh-cooked fish and
licked the can opener.

Source of wonder

City fountain in a dusty square
Baroque, reptilian, topped by floozies,
Early bath for lunchtime loafers
Mist and smoke swirl through the air.

Dangle feet in soapy foam,
Ice cream leftovers, lollipop sticks,
Copper coins too deep to reach,
And Cryptosporidiosis.

Pouting dolphins pulse and spit
Scaly serpents hiss and spray
Unicorns flaunt twisted horns
Moistened by the breeze blown spume.

In damp disgust we turn for home
To wonder what a fountain's for?

Jonathan Hill

Miss Fenton

Eng Lit taught by Miss Fenton in
serious but fashionable specs,
trim Jaeger cardigans

fringed with flowing skirts
billowing round her bike, she
pushed us naughty children firmly

 like the pedals, with insistent grace,
 our mentor with an empathetic face.
What's more, she knew we owned
an earthy humour best not shared.

We were so brash, so vulgar,
 lacking patience or remorse.
Miss Fenton's mind was on a higher plane, of course.

At the tennis court she proved her grit,
fine boned ankles dancing to the net,
high paced volleys packed with guile and steel,
overhead smashes backed – by gasps and frills.

Medal from Hell

Our French teacher won the Military Cross.
Sardonic, saturnine, poised, composed,
We never learned what bravery he'd shown
Nor could imagine hells that he'd endured.

Teased us with sarcastic epigrams
"You should learn English" was his best advice.
We travailed with unseen translation
Perfect French reduced to broken Anglo Saxon.

Patiently he bore our peasant prose,
His preference might have been for courtly Latin.
Betrayed his chagrin in a singular way,
Jingling loose change trousered in his flannels.

Each week a conscript, posted to the front,
Stood trembling at the blackboard in a dusty classroom
Asked to write a passage following dictation
Unworthy boy or girl exposed to deep humiliation.

Correcting every howler transcribed by a fool,
Sometimes Mr Meacham allowed himself...to smile.

Jonathan Hill

Time tellers

Spiky as a porcupine,
Gothic as Big Ben the park clock stands
ornate in corporation green.

Topped by cube-shaped head
each face braving one of four winds,
 each pair of hands
 keeping pace to a different drum.

More faithful
than our four faced liar,
the five o'clock bull bellows time for home.

Father's advice ignored

Ten years old that very day; top gift?
Complete fleet of Grand Prix Dinky cars.

Maserati hot and red, fancy Ferrari - yellow and blue.
Alfa Romeo, Talbot Lago, an HWM that went brumbrum,
And a no chance Cooper Bristol in British Racing Green.

Tony's mom had robbed her bank account to spoil me
while Raymond's mom with much less cash to spare
and far more kids to feed, raided her purse to buy
just one Ferrari, snug in its box, for two and six.

Dad said "one day that single car
will out-perform the rest"
"Don't be daft" scorning best advice to
moth ball spare Ferrari for all eternity
so staged Grand Prix race,
scraped it round our yard from pole position.
Today that model costs a ton if boxed in mint condition.

Jonathan Hill

Switch on the lights

Saturday afternoon, autumn sun,
mosaic: black shorts, gold shirts,
arms tattooed or un-inked,
faces printed individually
with dismay or ecstasy.

Thirty thousand football supporters
arms and fingers flashing
like silver birch coppice.

From those trees, a beast of a noise -
singular shouts aggregated in stereo
full-throated blasts of worship…wonder…woe.

Best those anthems sung in raucous concert,
once, "The Happy Wanderer" now
"Hi! Ho! Wolverampton."

Rampton alrightcha!
Mad about football -
brutal, elegant, infuriating.

Come dusk, sixty thousand feet rumble,
Drumming terraces
Floodlights enter stadium
Like visitors from another galaxy.

Lost Matchbox

Hit a matchbox down the street,
Kick it with your boots
Kick it with your feet
Hear it rattle, what's inside?
E's or weed or cyanide?

Chip the matchbox with your toe
Hear it rustle, see it fly
Off the kerb across the tar
Bouncing like a bent jam jar.

Crush the box, hear dying gasp
From buckled, battered, guts within,
Pick it up, take closer look,
Contents read like a comic book.

Some mug left fifty quid inside
Now he's planning…. suicide.
Hit a matchbox down the street
Kick it with your boots
Kick it with your fffffffeet.

Jonathan Hill

Pretending to be lifeguards...

Number 46

There's no bus like the last bus,
 unruly republic royalty rarely rides

Mine was a waltzing double decker
vibrant last dance partner
in green and yellow satin
under halogen streetlights

Her progress orchestrated by
uncompromising Mr Singh
blue turban, strictly tied,
armed with who knows what
beneath his corporation uniform?

Conductor - Carlton Campbell
Harry Belafonte doppelganger
dances stairs to upper deck
confronted by gang of dandies
menacing as rabid dogs,
whiff of Brylcreamed quiffs,
fag smoke, sweaty Saturday suits...

"Your tickets please! Your tickets please!"
Carlton's sharp falsetto cuts the night

"It's now or never,
my love won't wait!"

Teddy boys bark back the chorus,
pay their fares, little thinking Elvis too
some day will catch the last bus.

Jonathan Hill

Holiday Romance

Your pretence at wealth was crazy,
lacing overtures with French…
c'est la vie and mon amour
just ruse to speed seduction
and those pricey sunglasses
midnight blue, mysterious mirrors…

deep tanned skin, exotic lure,
curves and contours had me tangoed…
voice to lull a Yorkshire terrier
or deceive a customs officer...
all reasons why I sank so fast
onto my knees, down on couch.

wooed with warm words by a poseur
leaving me first beached then wrecked.

Pretending to be lifeguards...

We swept the sun-baked sand for girls
Who might be bored with life.

Careless, sun creamed lasses
Unchaperoned, unwary
All we asked was: "Can you swim?"

Whether yes or no, just "mind the rocks"
Putting some con into
our conversation.

Edged to common ground
"You on holiday then,
Where you from?"

If from the North
We came from London
Or vice versa.

"Borrow our li-lo?
It's all pumped up.
I'll hold it steady, you climb aboard."

With an eye to sunset
We enquired
"What's the food like at your hotel?"

"Thought so, why not meet us
For a drink tonight.
And huevos y fritos?"

Yes we spoke the Spanish.
"Adios and hasta la vista,
See you later alligator!"

"Don't forget to mind the rocks
Best avoid the local lads
They've no respect for English girls."

Jonathan Hill

Classics department night out

It seemed a good idea
to start with large gin slings
then to Caesar's wine bar

(enough for a Roman army)
loose talk, lascivious, salacious
 first sotto voce, later a fortiori

Tempers calmed by dolmades and courgette balls
in Titan taverna, with much Mythos beer

At last a rum nightcap in a rum night club,
then one for the street. Now, what was it?

Trip in the garden

Last night, exotic lanterns lit our path

red and orange firebrands fought the dark

earthy tang spiced southern breezes

dizzy senses span towards hallucination.

Took breath, stared again with steady gaze

discerned not torches but nasturtians,

we picked and bit each flaming bloom

relished signal colours and acidic musk

Tongues curled, hearts pumped

floral aphrodisiacs, fresh plucked,

drew snakes, green and slender,

across the crazy paving.

Delving…

Innocence strolls a curious path
Mystery entrance traps the gaze
(whose haunt or hide or haven?)

private portal to cell or den?
Deep within, faint fluttering...
instinct peers down narrow jaws

like dentist probing wobbly molar,
channel through some spindled roots,
throat's end, pool of blood, or water?

Weak half-light hints at hidden mirrors,
reflected flutters, frantic, flirtatious?
Burrow thatched with tangled twigs, dry grass

twisted with last winter's spiky holly,
pricks still threaten skin, do not dare
insert a finger, let alone a limb.

Flickers beckon, hands retreat
eyes pry, no respect to privacy
for net-trapped and half-butchered fly

twitching on web in final throes
nor else squat toad,
throbbing, ill-perfumed, and parched

pining for an April douche?
No, none of the above. another shiver,
flash of black and gold reveals

tight belt across round bellied bumble bee
hovering like midnight bouncer...
one mystery solved, but why so busy under cover?

Rugby team at prayer

Dry March day, toward season's end

On benches and chairs borrowed from assembly

2nd fifteen mustered for eternal photograph

PE teacher Mr Savage aching for a cigarette

Headteacher Mr Chambers, plotting character formation

William Short, five feet tall, begging for extra inches

John Long, over two yards high, pleading for new shorts

Nikolai Adamski looking forward... to chess club

Trevor Stubbs looking forward... to Jennifer Careless

Clarence Yardley rehearsing dubious jokes

And Frankie Finn fearing his father's temper.

In front row, as deceitful as life itself,

Unbiddable oval ball squats on a sturdy lap.

Jonathan Hill

Kalani Pan

Swimming at Christmas 1969

East of Lusaka, west of Chainama Hills
that was the year we swam till sundown
under an awning of cotton blue sky.

Surprised by water's clinging warmth and
yellow swallowtails, large as small birds,
settling to drink from poolside puddles.

Bitter-sweet scent, high savannah grass in flame,
stirring senses dizzied by whirring crickets, and
dulled by Christmas pudding.

Out of the pool, on heat-heavy patio,
a rainbow array of flip flops spreads ready to
shield pink feet from the occasional scorpion.

Jonathan Hill

Hark!

Hot day dawns, whistles and drums
from Shilinga township
seven small soldiers bring festive greetings,
dresses and trousers ndeleshi, ntoloshi, worn to tatters
 bare foot dancers without nzapatas
raise red dust.

Beating out hell, overlaying harmony,
drums, kankobelas, thumb pianos
little virtuosos plucking
tin box guitars.

Fat white foreigners
muzungu mafuta
hail kids surviving
 on one meal a day - Merry Christmas!

Beware of the dog, nchenjerani ndi galu
with one loud yap, hounds hang back
soft morning air, franjipani scent,
threaded by throbs and songs
strums and twangs.

Zicomo, Zicomo, Zicomo Kwambili
Thank you, thank you, thank you very much,
Small coins clatter into battered pan
Gifts exchanged, musicians march on.

ndeleshi = dresses   ntoloshi = trousers
nzapatas = shoes   kankobelas = thumb pianos
muzungu = white person; literally "aimless wanderer"
nchenjerani ndi galu = literally "be clever of the dog!"
zicomo kwambili = thank you very much

Kalani Pan

If you should ever reach Kalani Pan
Through tall savannah grass and high ant hills
Greet with great respect the village men.

Life there is hungry, short and hard,
Not much to eat nor drink…nothing to read
If you should ever reach Kalani Pan.

Perhaps they still smelt metal by the glowing ton,
Charcoal, charms and bellows feeding fire,
Greet with great respect the village women.

Blacksmiths sing to phantoms *run rock run*,
Be wary of furnaces that crack!
Should ever you reach Kalani Pan.

Bartered trade, metal block and creamy tusk
Once spread far from continent to coast so
Greet with great respect the old headman.

Elephant all vanished from the veld,
Ore has shrunk, benefits dispersed….
But if you ever reach Kalani Pan,
Offer my regrets to the old headman.

Jonathan Hill

Instructions from a Weaver Bird

Tie knot, fix string of grass to vacant branch
but first locate a tree

At end of string construct a ring around a secure perch
first sing ear-splitting trills, heat-piercing notes

Harvest a thousand strips of grass, weave basket hung from string
but first anticipate a mate

Finish the basket roundly in full geometric form
plan to add a short cylindrical horn...

Such an entrance to the nest will baffle birds of prey...
flutter yellow wings and invite a friendly hen

Flaunt handsome mustard coat and black masked face...
but should your green grass love nest fade too soon
prospective wives will simply turn you down

If a hen approves your weaver's craft
Nature will complete.... the work of art.

Sea Harvest

Gritty shells sprinkled with salt sea sand
Empty shells echoing white surf sounds

Oysters prised from rugged armour,
Symmetrical scallops dressed for dinner

Razors syphoning plankton food
Malodorous barnacles from estuary mud

Winkle homes vacant for hermit crabs
Shocking pink flashes on tide's last lap

Arranged on windowsill, mirrored in glass,
Holiday finds, reminders of loss.

Jonathan Hill

Sea Field

Under restless sky, sharp green grassland
vimmed in winter with powdered snow, scoured by wind from
every compass point, especially westwards.
Caithness and Sutherland, North West across the Moray Firth.

Great gales emerge as though from Lossiemouth,
varieties of cloud - black-inked thunderers, sparse white cirrus.
Come summer Sea Field's lightning-struck then sun- baked
as Russian steppes, revived in autumn by pin-sharp rain.

Fishing boats stay in port while weather forecasts
test the height of Admiral Beaufort's scale, yet
Scandic Fieldfare in hundreds once made landfall safely
on Sea Field. Purposeful, grey-mottled birds, strong yellow beaks.
 Northern visitation of mistle thrush relations,
 'schack, schack' calls, thick feathers mocking outlook.

Fieldfare survive on berries, intrepid insects, wiry worms, corn
escaped from threshing.
Congregations now decline, where once there had been
multitudes. Less food for grazing through December.

Something at sea might consume fallen Fieldfare, or some
scrawny beast
from furze fringed hedge carry their carrion back for supper.

Will many Fieldfare fly next year to winter, on Sea Field?
Count them on the fingers of two hands.

The vigilant shopkeeper

Hockey stick at elbow, Mr Patel
sees heavy men pad by

his well-stocked store,
plastic toys, cooking oil and coriander.

Shop counter rippled with red tops,
wave on wave of triviality and spite.

Perhaps those men conceal screwdrivers and
baseball bats under bulky jackets?

Behind the till a charity box and bags of Bombay Mix.
Across door's blind, shadows insinuate.

Two strangers enter, make enquiries, offer protection,
surprise visit by the Leeds Police.

The grieving traveller

Time blinks, stops, falters, starts
when tragedy occurs,
swooping without warning,
like scavengers or birds of prey.

Breathing must be restored
to fill with air
lungs tightly packed with shock,
restart the pump that's paused.

When worst befalls,
we might not even hear wings beat
nor notice fateful raptors in grey sky
nor sense a chilling flurry.

Instead someone might gently,
(or even not so gently) say
I don't know how to share
such appalling news.

Life for many then moves on
but not quite yet for you,
tears leak… then pour.

Solitary places bleed sounds
never made before nor since,
medieval beaks score skin
flint-sharp talons penetrate heart.

Were grief to shade your path
along the road of life,
a more complete traveller you'll become
despite losing that which you most highly prize.

When a pale child is called away
the loss is fixed by flightless birds
riding backs, scarring shoulders
torturing composure,
unwelcome companions
on every journey
until, until, until.....

Our Local…

Long lunch in Leicester

Let us wander on New Walk, by trees and past squares,
So near to the city....so far from its cares.
Meet streams of scholars, a street drinking crew,
With couples and coppers and nuns rolling through.

    Museum portico, guarded with cannon,
    Marvel at dinosaurs' fossicked neck bones.
    From the office at lunch we'll launch a long break,
    In the Kings Head we'll gather, strong beers to knock back.

        No horses, carriages... vehicles verboten,
        No trams, cabs nor cars, no noises sudden.
        In New Walk we're safe from sirens and wheels,
        Let's buy a Big Issue – check out its appeal.

We'll berth at the Belmont on our homeward tack.
Crisps the right ballast to sober up Jack.
We'll sail back to work from two until five,
A blue army chant warns the boss we've arrived!
Long after dark if you're wanting a fight,
The prison is looming just out of sight.

    Svelte lawyers mince past at three seconds to three,
    Creep into their chambers for shortbread and tea.
    Through Georgian windows some residents peep,
    living in New Walk will never be cheap.

        Yet every newcomer under the sun
        can follow this path and count it as home.
        From Victoria Park to Welford Square,
        Leicester embodies a way to share.

Jonathan Hill

When questioned...

You do not have to say anything
But it may harm your defence
If you do not mention something
You later rely on in evidence.

You can say you said nothing
But don't depend on anything,
Or they might question you
And extract the whole truth.

Do not rely on Morse
Or you will fall asleep, of course.
In Oxford if you disclose evidence
You cannot rely on Lewis' intelligence.

Should you fall asleep in the nick
And wake up with Frost
You will be crossly examined
Until you confess.

If Taggart mutters something
It might mean murder.
Better prepare your defence
Before you enter the tenements.

So when cautioned, state your alibi,
But do not mention revenge,
Or later in the dock
It may harm your innocence.

Anything you do say
May be taken down
And used by the cops
In the tv lounge.

Jack the Glazier

God's time-served glazier worked his tools last night,
installed ferny features in our windows
inscribed frosty fractals on smooth cold glass
white silk curtains blinding every pane.

By noon, clear views of bare fields reappear,
sparrows peck ice-hardened water,
red winter sun already glowing fit to set,
and all the garden dreaming…
of long warm days ahead.

Jonathan Hill

The Hunters

Slender dog-like shadow on the Fosse
russet brown a cunning camouflage
scavenger for roadkill, nurturer of cubs,
long tail trailing in the winter dusk.

Salient, that silvered evening were the ears
erect, alert, attuned to every chance and risk,
dawn revealed a slim sly fox still there,
still and dead, with only one ear pricked.

Quick sharp ear appears to flicker
troubled by a litter's anxious screams,
mother's spirit calls across the valley…
don't wait for me..don't wait for me.

Buzzard flies out from his thorny perch
over the hedge and fast along the Fosse
streamlined, hungry, ready to kill and feast
pinpointing where to strike, to slice live meat.

Pavement on Meadow

Take a walk from Quorn to Barrow
on paving laid in water meadows.

Set close by the River Soar
slabs stretch half a mile or more,
surrounded by soft murmuring grass,
fields of forage fed by floods.

When rain has rinsed the cold, hard stones,
surface shimmers, clean as new,
high-peaked pylons frame our view.

Amphibians discharge their spawn
runners and ramblers turn by turn
trickle through the claggy marsh,
(you might yet need your stick or staff).

Slabs are raised or cracked or sunk
briskly tread both rough and smooth
best put some old trainers on
to pace the children if they run.

Cattle, seagulls, herds and flocks,
swans in pairs, dogs in packs
all give chase to keep us warm.

Liveried narrow boats in line,
fly flapping flags of pants and jeans,
through River Soar's black tannic brew
throbbing engines stir and screw.

Jonathan Hill

But though *our* aim is straight and narrow
to well-fed Quorn from bony Barrow,
mobile homes on timber decks
wink temptation in the dusk.

Will orange sunsets tint the scene,
to light fresh grass where willows lean?

Or knotted serpents hiss, spit, sigh,
Along the lea where flagstones lie?

Instructions from a Weaver Bird   41

Over a Barrel

Beneath the lintel stands landlord Tom,
swollen feet a universe of pangs and pain,
above his head, engraved in gilded lettering:
"licensed" - to slowly poison faithful friends.

Takes his pick from tangle headed rock
musicians looking for a place to gig,
discovers big-boned wide-eyed bar staff talent,
thirsty dray men clock his knowing wink.

Tom Wadham's in this world for other people
dispensing both refreshment and advice,
tempting even those who should know better -
 "Why not try another golden pint?"

Masterful in cellars dark and cool,
Tom changes barrels in the nick of time,
servile in the shadow of his partner Joan,
she who cooks the books and feeds the famished swine.

Socks

Memorable statue, serene, seraphic,
Market-place shoppers touch your toes for luck
Erstwhile target for widespread resentment
now embraced with warm affection

Bouldery presence: foot outstretched,
socks embellished with zigs and zags,
leaf laid in lap for vital privacy

Sculptor, Glaswegian Shona Kinloch
perhaps better known for dogs than socks.

Smooth-surfaced monument
verdigris patina
poised on plinth beside town hall,
buying satsumas, we touch your toes for luck.

Fate of a Poet

Jonathan Hill

Shed in Nanpantan

In western corner of our garden, a moss-clad shed,
my refuge for sulking on a rainy day,
amid the flimsy geometry of spider webs
a small fly hangs, shrink-wrapped for supper.

Rusty tools with handles still intact,
remnant rolls of poppy wallpaper,
cans of creosote, unused emulsion tins
rest on containers of distemper and shellac.

Beyond this hideout lies a rotting compost heap
of grudges and regrets not quite yet buried,
mumbled apologies, unshared and so past useful now,
unfinished business from life's long agenda.

All beneath an evergreen and aromatic tree,
scattering redemptive leaves, across an unmown lawn.

Salt

Mined and refined in England or India,
Savoury perk for Roman soldiers,
Shaken on fish and chips with warm brown vinegar,
Miracle reviver of a cold meat lunch.

Or in hard blue twists of greaseproof paper
To tumble carelessly in packets of crisps,
Thirst increasing with every crunch,
Salt grain desiccating drinkers' lips.

Or in large lorry loads at the side of hills
On winter days when new snow falls.
Mixed with grit to spread across highways,
Surface sandpapered, frost to forestall.

Seasoning the spray from a Yarmouth tide,
 Or in pinches sprinkled on Sunday dinners,
Dependable, crystalline, pure and white,
Dissolved in tears….at dead of night.

Jonathan Hill

Red Rock House

Not built up from blocks nor bricks
but chiselled out from rosy sandstone cliffs
first cave, then house, concealed in rock

Rock, soft to excavate and tinted softly too:
carnelian red, rust rouge, smoked salmon pink,
colonised by emerald moss and troglodytes.

Before Christ, people found homes here
until 1963: dwelling declared unfit,
the Council in its wisdom put a stop to it.

Duly re-opened by the National Trust,
visitors gawp, scoff scones, sip tea,
above them, strata sag like sliced gateaux.

Enter, find smooth rounded corners, nothing square,
one cell's ceiling graced by concave hollow
room for tall loud clock to chime each hour

Mary's war

"What was it like in the war, Mary?"
Just great said Mary to me.
Our sales rep joined the navy
'Cos he'd never seen the sea.

The gaffer put me on the road,
I went out in the firm's little car,
Travelled on business to Stoke in the north....
It seemed loike ever so far.

Some days wuz just bostin', in my shoiny Austin
I'd set out quite early you see,
Get there for me breffus in Darlaston
Visit Stan's place in Tipton for tea.

I'd stop for some drinks in a pub
A mild, then a black-market gin,
Charmed me customers inside out,
Got back as me husband got in.

Then he was called up to serve,
 I stayed calm and carried roight on
Driving to Brumagen down in the south,
Visiting friends in West Brom.

One day the gaffer declared
"Yo'm y-goin' to Wales next wik"
"But it's too far for me to get wum by dark!"
"That's alroight, I'll come with you. What cheek!"

Jonathan Hill

Still in Wales we could get some fresh fish,
Or mebbe a lean joint of lamb,
If business went well, we'd stay overnoight,
It'd all mek a noice change from Spam.

Then peace broke out,
and me husband cum back.

He wuz all sugar and spoice,
Just loike our honeymoon over again,
Yes, the war it was ever so noice!

Headgear

When my wife acquires a hat it makes me feel
important: a feeling that I hate
unless she wears a hat.

What kind of hat does she actually buy?
Well, I haven't honestly got a clue.

And has my wife a lot of hats?
 No idea – it's quite a few...
she probably has more shoes
than hats– what's it to you?

Me? I have no hats at all
just two pairs of shoes..
one Sienna leather, another charcoal suede,
both pairs go with my chinos
which once were powder blue.

 I'm not a well-dressed kind of guy,
while my wife's apparel's fine from top to toe.
I feel so sophisticated when
she decides to sport a hat.

But wonder why she chooses
quite so many shoes...?

Jonathan Hill

July

One strange year the weather crystallised,
calendars stalled and August never came.

July delphiniums, blue but brittle,
grew and bloomed past January's end.

Christmas lupins decorated festive
rooms in mauve and pink to welcome visitors.

Wisteria smothered windows, dahlias clogged gutters,
explanations for weird weather, unsettlingly dour.

We cursed St Swithun's blessed name,
perhaps he thought a greedy world needed warnings
 more severe than a little extra rain.

By mid-April, orange crocus, better late than never,
final warning 'til snow falls,.. perhaps for ever.

Fate of a Poet

They've cleared out number forty four,
books, bedding, furniture and dust
framed photograph by Fay Godwin
carelessly chucked in transit van.

Last sighting of that man next door,
sagging chins, snooty nose,
pompous cheeks, famous but fascistic eyes,
goodbye at last to those sneering lips.

Dear departed neighbour, poisoner
of cats, feckless planter of Leylandii
his artful portrait by Ms Godwin
clumsily tumbrilled to the tip.

Jonathan Hill

Small Print Blues

Dear Mr Hemingway,
dear Mr Hemingway
you're seeking insurance
you're seeking insurance
to protect against risks
on a snowy day.

Dear Mr Hemingway,
Before we consider you
Gotta let our underwriters
have their say.

Excluded from most policies are
hazardous activities with
handguns, Daiquiri or
kissing female lips.

We don't cover air travel,
hunting in Africa
brawling, civil war or
loss of manuscripts.

Lacking no claims bonuses
premiums shoot sky high
even if you check the box
for voluntary excess
for voluntary excess

Dear Mr Hemingway
thank you for your letter
(received today from Idaho)
underwriters' views are non-negotiable,
regretfully in your case
the decision is no!